TWENTY YEARS

TWENTY YEARS

JOHN C. HARRELL

with art
by
Philip L. "Moki" Martin

LIGHTNING PUBLICATIONS
1992

Copyright © 1992 John C. Harrell
Illustrations © 1992 Philip L. Martin
All Rights Reserved

The poems and artwork in this book are protected individually and collectively by the copyright laws of the United States of America and shall not be reproduced in any manner whatever without express permission of the author or his designated representatives.

Lee Mallory, Editor

Cover Art, "Flags" by P.L. "Moki" Martin
Cover Design by Richard Lyon Clark

Previous Publications:

Some of the poems in this book were first published in the *Los Angeles Times, Journal of the Gulf War, The Orange County Register, Petyls,* and *Women Marines Association Newsletter.*

LIGHTNING PUBLICATIONS
532 South Raymond Avenue
Fullerton, California 92631
(714) 879-8300

ISBN-0-9632702-2-2

These poems are dedicated
to Tee
and
to Captain Ofelia Vicent, who wanted to know.

A FOREWORD TO *TWENTY YEARS*

The lion speaks. In a foreword to a collection of my own work, Charles Bukowski wrote that the master poet should "wait on the word." John Harrell has waited. Though these extraordinary poems could have come sooner, the tragic and poignant experience of war is better rendered for the wait. Rendered with tact and care.

The majority of these poems boil up in a fiery swirl of pain from twenty years past. The smoky magma of an incandescent cauldron–poems like tracers fired through a long night. Nevertheless, there's a tenderness here, too, where after a deep sleep, the poems bubble up in an unconscious flowering. The lion speaks.

Harrell's experience as well as his eye is profound. As he writes, "God I pray/when I aim to kill him . . . /that my shot is clean/that he does not suffer needlessly" – we sense the poet's arrival at life's absolute. Moreover, these poems sing with artistry, a psychic scaffolding upholding and upheld by experience.

Our poet is a humble man. War does that to men like John who fought to save lives. So, too, is he a thoughtful man. As the late Kenneth Rexroth once told me, "Recollection in tranquility produces a maximum of individuality." Ironically, he continued, – "Potential is lost when one attempts to turn it into power" – a veritable footnote to war.

John Harrell is a quiet, good and honest man. And perhaps in his voice and in these times, these poems finally play "Taps" for soldiers' quiet and harrowing dilemma. Beyond that long "wait on the word," the lion speaks.

Lee Mallory
Newport Beach

AUTHOR'S ACKNOWLEDGEMENTS

I wish to thank Valarie Prince, who taught me the freedom and Lee Mallory, mentor and editor who taught me the tools.

In addition, I would like to thank the generous friends who have helped me through this collection with their encouragement and knowledge: Nancy Rayl, Mary J. Andrews, Deborah E. Plummer, Brigadier General Harold H. Shively, Lieutenant Colonel John Porter, and last but not least, Master Sergeant Ken Raatz, a professional soldier in every sense.

CONTENTS

Prologue

In 1965 1
(untitled) 2
N V A Woman 3
The Lieutenant 4
The New Man 5
(untitled) 6
Fever of an Unknown Origin 7
A Child 8
H & I 9
Ducks 10
Nine–Thirty 11
(untitled) 12
The Chinook 13
Dopers 14
The Supply Sergeant 15
Thoughts at a Hockey Game 16
Medics 17
(untitled) 18
(untitled) 19
Alone 20
(untitled) 21
Calls 22
Drops 23

The Gulf War

(untitled) 24
Soldiers 25
The Scent 26
7 Dec 90 27
(untitled) 28
(untitled) 29
The Prayer 30
Flags 31
Two Poems 32
The Storm 33
(untitled) 34
(untitled) 35

The Other Wars
The Tree 36
(untitled) 37
Women Warriors 38
War 39
Vanishing 40
(untitled) 41
Love Child 42
(untitled) 43
Dacotah 44
Staff Sergeant B 45
To Jane 46
The Game 47
David 48
Managua Haiku 49
(untitled) 50
Pigs 51
This War 52

After The Wars
Near One Year 53
"The Triple Nickel" 54

PROLOGUE

Simmering, simmering like a witch's caldron
Twenty years.
Sometimes boiling, burning my soul
Destroying my family, my friends,
My mind.
At other times, just there
Just below the surface.
Only a scratch away, a look.
Memories of Vietnam.
Of people, places, events,
No disclaimer needed, because
I could never remember their names.

I worked underground,
With underground people.
We saved lives when we could.
Maybe your life.
I apologize to you if I should,
We tried to save you all,
Sometimes too well.
Sometimes not well enough.

It's taken twenty years,
A generation.
Maybe now it's simmered enough.

30 March 1990

IN 1965

IN 1965

On a quiet night,
Hushed voices talked above the sea.
The ship moved towards their destination.
Lighted cigarettes blinked
Summer breezes touched sweating hands.

"Two in ten," they said,
Those, the odds.
Of those nine hundred,
Only one hundred eighty would die.

A radio on the bridge gave background noise
Feet shuffled across cargo hatches, coughs
Not loud, no loud noises that night.

One hundred eighty,
What right have we to deny them.
The South China Sea was silent against their muffled voices,
"What right have we? What right have we?"
"In *Crito* lies the answer, in *Crito*," I said.
"But what if he is wrong!" they cried.
I could not answer, I would not answer.
I still can't answer.

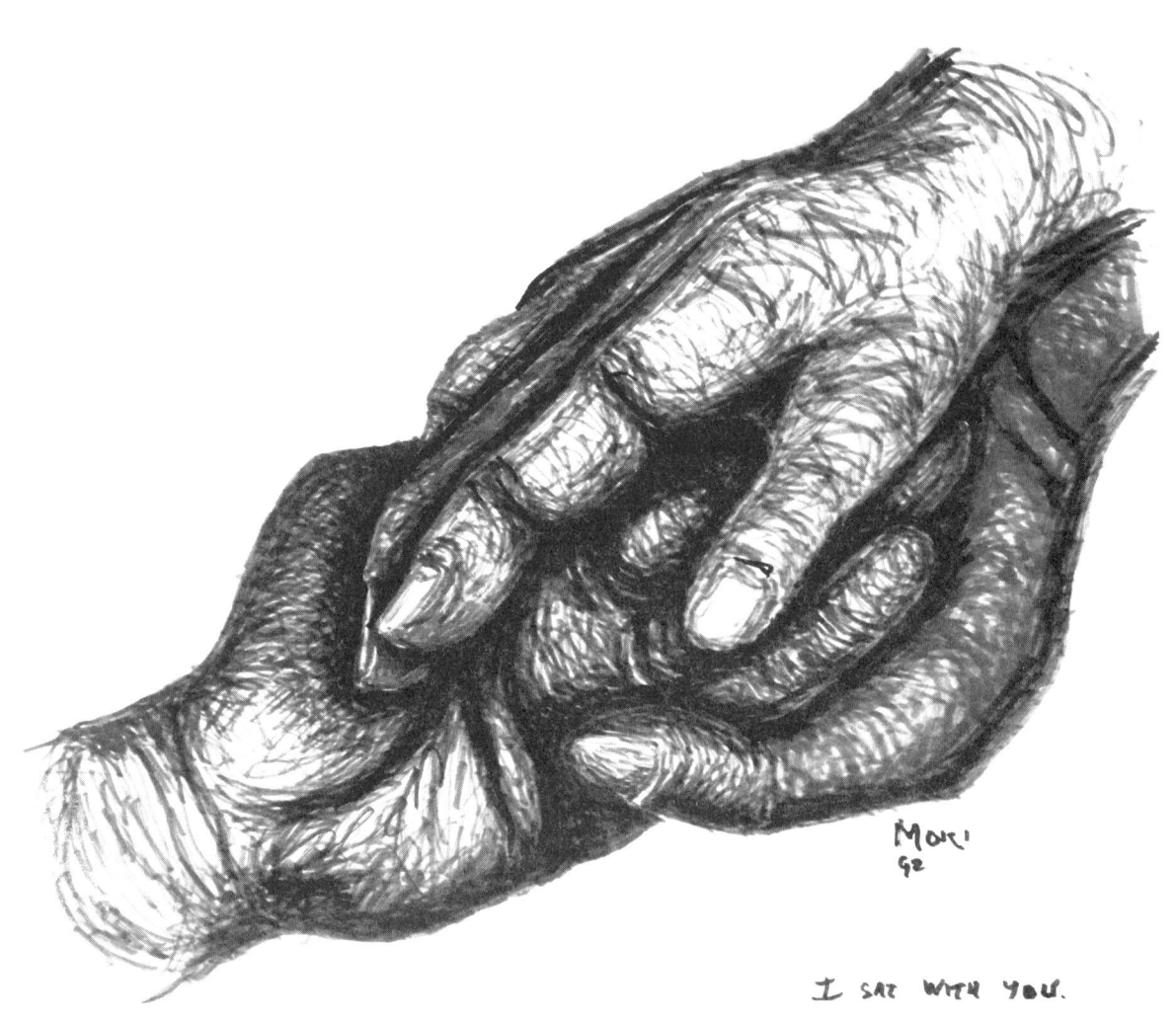

I sat with you.

(Untitled)

I sat with you and cried.
It was 10 or 11, you hadn't died yet.
It wasn't said, "He's going to die." But we knew.
The doctors were busy, we had four others.
Your brain half exploded.
I held your hand, wondered, who are you?
But I wouldn't look at your dog tags.
I thought of your family, how lonely they'd be.
I held your hand, no one should die alone,
In an empty corner.
I imagined your life,
Happy on a farm in Ohio, or maybe Iowa.
I don't know why, but I knew you'd been happy.
Yours was a simple face, a simple life, a simple death.
You never knew, you never felt it, a fragment probably.
Why you?

In 30 minutes you died officially.
They came and got you.
More patients, always more,
I went back to work.

N V A WOMAN

They brought you in dying.
Damn, women don't die fighting.
What were you doing?
Why?
Two .50 caliber hits,
One in the right thigh,
One below the left knee.
Your legs were ribbons of meat.
How can a body tear so.
You had an AK–47 they said,
Running, firing.
Why?
I can't let you die.
Delicate face, small,
Beautiful once.
I took your leg below the knee,
What was left.
I stopped the flow, I bound you,
I cleaned you.
Others did more.
We gave you blood
Life's blood, our blood
8 pints. I never saw
Someone drink so much.
We tried, we tried so hard.
Then you left, another place
Better care, a hospital.
I felt good, you were alive.
In hours I called,
I had to know
Were you O.K., what would happen to you?
"The N V A woman," they said
"O she died. We had to keep her in
A hallway 'till the American surgeries were done."
And now, who will remember you
N V A Woman?

THE LIEUTENANT

They put him in the next bed,
The young Lieutenant.
He was asleep
Peaceful.
You couldn't tell
Watching him
That an AK–47 round
Had taken a road trip
Through his body.
Entering his left thigh
Hitting bone
Accelerating up
Through his bowels
His stomach
Into his rib cage
Slowly turning past
His heart, out of control
Smashing into a rib
On his right side
Exploding out his back.
A ride through
A Grand Canyon.

The General came
In all his glory
Mumbling the words,
While his Aide felt around
In a paper sack
For another Purple Heart.

The next afternoon
He opened his eyes,
Asking
Am I going home?
Yes.
He went back to sleep,
Peaceful sleep.

THE NEW MAN

I met you the day I left on R & R.
A fresh face, clean, 18–19 from somewhere.
I enjoyed Hawaii.
My family, my son, the sea.
I didn't think of you,
I didn't worry.
We had experienced medics.
"Bad Karma," they'd say.
Five days, back into that smell,
That country.
Some flyboy in Da Nang complained to me,
"No fresh vegetables again today."
While we kept body bags in our reefer.
A first convoy, nothing complex.
A pressure mine, nothing complex.
How could you die?
I didn't even know you.
Your records said "Protestant."
But that holy man couldn't understand what happened,
So we had the Soldier's Priest read instead.
Does it really matter to God?
Rest, rest
I hope in your next life
Your Karma's better.

(Untitled)

What a shot.
I read the toe tag again,
"Shot by an AMERICAL sniper,
575 yds."
Clean through and through,
Amazing.
He couldn't be more than 12.

FEVER OF AN UNKNOWN ORIGIN

Always the eyes
Watching you,
As you move
From part to part
Around the canvas stretcher.

Stump of an arm,
Ankle,
Cut away the foot
Held by a piece
Of nothing.
Gauze four–by–fours
In handfuls
Filling holes,
Stopping blood
More blood,
Your blood.

Now I lay here
Wet
Shirt clinging
Pillow stinking
Wet
At 2:30
On a November night
Wondering why
You infected me with
A fever of unknown origin
Too.

A CHILD

What a terrible place to have a baby.
Men are dying here
Faces gone
Pieces of souls splattered
On walls
Floors.
Pain of the living,
Each day more pain.

In your small fragile body
You have a life.
Why would you want to bring a son,
A daughter into this hell?
This damning place.

Have they lived
These twenty years
In comfort, warmth or torment?
Who are they now?
Is it you by the fountain
Studying history?

H & I (Harassment and Interdiction)

We sat at night
Watching the artillery fires.
The lumination rounds, tracers
Like bony fingers reaching out,
Searching, finding some unknown heart.
Exploding light bouncing off misting clouds
Eerie, the distant thunder of the impacts.
A symphony of sight and sound,
Whose ending may be nothing
Maybe death. A hand, a leg
That marks that place.
We would chase the parachutes from small flares,
Laughing, drinking, not thinking.
All night long, at random times, at random places they would fire.
We would drink and laugh,
Drink and laugh,
Drink.

DUCKS

He was drinking coffee,
The CID man.
We sat and talked,
We tried to understand,
23 that month.
23 times an AMERICAL man tried or killed another.
They called it "Fragging."
But it wasn't always a grenade,
Sometimes a shot in the back, a shot in the dark.
How did one explain that at home?
He was an asshole.
He got his men killed.
He was a lousy leader.
He just pissed me off.
23 times that month,
It must have been June.
We drank coffee, we talked.

I remembered the "F Troop" ISt SGT.
It was self-defense,
Through the heart he shot him
At 50 feet. His response to the threat.

My response was ducks.
Nature's sentinels and a .45.
I slept soundly.
I tried to tell my replacement,
Take care of them,
But within a month they'd been eaten,
And another month
Men had to guard him.
Maybe he was just a sonofabitch.
But me,
I had my ducks.

NINE–THIRTY

They brought you in that morning
At nine–thirty.
A small wound,
But you knew.

A severed artery in your leg.
Simple, easy to save.
Yet you knew before us,
We wouldn't believe.

What else was severed at nine–thirty?
You watched us work in silence.
Your eyes followed us. Why wouldn't
You speak?

At nine–forty you died.
Not of the wound we saw,
Something else.
Why wouldn't you help us?

(Untitled)

Don't get on the lead track.
It's the one that gets you killed.
A contact mine,
Then ambush.
Fire and smoke,
Pieces of men,
That smell.
I walk to the head of the column.

The road, a trail.
Searing heat, sweat
Burning my eyes.
A .50 ready,
Gut scared.
Why is he smiling at me?
I mean to kill him.
Don't get on the lead track.

THE CHINOOK

I was used to the Hueys.
When they came
They only brought
Three or four at a time.
If it was bad,
Maybe nine.
Those pilots had balls.
I could handle nine
We all could.
Then the Chinook came.

The Chinook
Opening its jaws like Jonah's whale.
Disgorging
Old men, old women
Children, babies
All shot, shot somewhere.
No men, just
Old and young.
Each hit in a different place.
Each a terrible wound.

I don't know
How many died
How many lived,
Even where they went.
Some to the ARVN Hospital
Some to District.
I couldn't keep track of the carnage.

What happened - a Viet Cong "My Lai."
Never in the paper
Not on anyone's radio.
Just another day
When the Chinook landed.

DOPERS

I hated dopers.
They were dangerous,
They got you killed or
Killed you.

At night Doc and I
Would sit on the roof
And watch their butts glow,
Like fireflies on a summer night.
He sipped scotch
I drank my buck fifty a fifth whiskey.
Between the outgoing 155 rounds,
We'd talk of women
And home.
Laughing we'd stagger off to bed.

Dopers know they're safe at night,
But my revenge was sweet.
Each day I'd go where fireflies flew
And find the 8-inch joints under the sandbags.
Then slowly I'd piss on each nestled cache,
Leaving them to dry for someone's use.
Christ, what a bladder I had.

Twelve years later
I got thrown out
Of a motel in Taos,
For smoking my Lady's finest home-grown
And tying her nightie
In a knot on the ceiling fan.

THE SUPPLY SERGEANT

He could have gone home.
I would have sent him.
He didn't belong
He was too old
His health was bad.
He should not have been sent.
I told him
Go.

He said no
I'll stay
Let me do my job.
He didn't belong.
He worked quietly,
Bringing in,
Building.

I never ask from where,
He would smile,
We grew. We prospered.
I would see
His bent weathered frame
That didn't belong
And he would say
"Keep on truckin'."

The bodies came and went
He kept on
Never complaining
Never asking – why
What's in it for me.
He went home finally,
This professional soldier.
A man who made
A difference.

THOUGHTS AT A HOCKEY GAME

Miss Jennifer Steele will now sing the National Anthem...

I should have shot you
You sonofabitch,
Like you said I would.
So-called surgeon, Major.
In truth butcher.
Your idea of war
British colonial movies.

We wouldn't let you touch the living,
You weren't worthy of the dead.
How many have you killed since?
Incompetent, uncaring, callous,
Thuggee.

You bastard
I wish this paper bullet
Could splatter your brain.

Kings 2 - Penguins 1
In overtime.

MEDICS

I had them both.
One a carpenter by trade.
He made beautiful furniture,
An artist with wood, quiet
He wanted to teach when he went home.

He'd been sent with F Troop,
A track outfit.
He was a pacifist,
A true pacifist.
Many medics claimed to be pacifists
But most weren't,
At least not after they'd been shot at.

He told me he'd trained
All his life to be a medic.
If there was a war,
He would be drafted.
It was the only way he could serve.
He did,
One of the best, gentle with patients
Caring, he knew what to do with pain.

After a week out with the tracks
Their Commander sent him back,
He was good, too good.
He slowed them down they said,
He treated the enemy.
He slowed them down.
I understood,
I should have argued,
But I needed good medics then too.

My other combat medic,
Also an F Troop man.
After his third Purple Heart
I wouldn't let him go out any more.
He was mad at me for awhile.
We put him in for a Silver Star,
He only received a Bronze Star,
With "V" device.
I guess it wasn't written well enough.
We all knew he deserved more
Much more.

CHOP-CHOP CHOPPING...

(Untitled)

A sound I hear
That always brings pain,
And although I love to fly,
Is the sound, that 'chop, chop, chopping'
Sound of the blades of a helicopter
Landing, taking off.
Of years ago,
When it fetched bodies to heal
      or beyond healing at times,
Brought pieces of men.
I hear the sound now
And remember then,
Always the 'chop, chop, chopping.'

(Untitled)

Kings Inn
21 Jan 1977

Seven years now,
The dust and dirt we worked in is gone.
In a clean bar,
Music in the background,
A fire, warm conversation.
Things you will never know.
Today they gave amnesty to those
    who would not come.
But you came
    and stayed.

I vowed that my son would
    not die like you
Or all the others.
But can I live his life?
No.
He must decide himself,
I must cut him loose.
Live, my son.

A father cried then at the news of the death of his son.
But at least his son lived his own life,
He served with honor.
He is remembered now,
On another sad day for
    his country.

ALONE

I am still alone,
I have not come home,
I've made no peace with my self.

There is a Wall, the names in black
Upon my mind, within the ground.
A time I did not understand haunts me still.

I only wanted to serve my country.
I am alone, betrayed.
I did my best, what more did you want?

11 November 1982, I drove 500 miles and found peace.
Within your arms I was safe, I could rest awhile.
Where do I run on the 21st of November?

11/82
J

(Untitled)

Where did they all go?
Not the men who died,
I know where they went,
But the men who lived.
The ones with no legs,
Or one arm,
One eye.
The man who sat holding his mangled hand,
Waiting patiently,
"Take my friends first," he said.
Where did they all go?
To Dallas, Pittsburgh, Deming, Ayer
What do they think?

We talk of the Wall, the names
In quiet reverence, awe.
But what of the others,
Where did they go?

CALLS
(Haiku)

Calls bring back visions,
Evenings of a winter moon,
Lonely sound of Taps.

Jan 82
J

DROPS

During some season
It rained
Each afternoon.
Hot steaming drops.

When the helicopters came
Drops of blood
Made beautiful mosaics
In the puddles.
Swirling, mixing
No two pools ever the same.
Some dark pomegranate
Some peppermint
Moving, changing.
Each man's blood blending
With his friends'
And foes'.

THE GULF WAR

(Untitled)

Here beast.
Let me rub you,
Give you our
Warm cream.
Feel you arch your back
Against my mind.
Watch your eyes cloud
With dreams of
More meat.

11 Nov 90
J

SOLDIERS

When you look
The horizon
Rocks, sand
Can be anywhere.

Without a face,
A voice
To give a clue,
It could be
Any land
You came to
Die in.

11 Nov 90
J

THE SCENT

The scent of war
Does strange things
To humans.
Instead of running in fear,
They seek to embrace
Its gory arms,
Feeling they become more manlike
Not less human.

7 DEC 90

This day
In another time
Eagles came screaming
Out of a morning sun,
Talons mauling
The unprotected flock.

What cost
Wrong avenged,
The world returned to its natural order.

Tears still shed
Memories dim
And other lambs
Prepare for terrible sacrifice,
While Kimberly makes coffee
At thirty thousand feet.

(Untitled)

How can I tell you goodbye?
I know where you go
The horror that may await you.
The pain, yours - theirs
The scar, real, imagined.

How can I tell you goodbye?
Gentle face, kindness
Full of love, giving.
It will destroy you
I know
No one stays unchanged,
Unfeeling.

How can I let you go?
My mind screams at you
    run, hide
Get away. Don't let them
Take you.

I smile gently
Holding your hand
Saying, "Take care
Come back safely."

7 Dec 90
For Capt Ofelia Vicent
J

(Untitled)

15 Jan 1991
1430

Reading words from the past,
Voices from the past
Are present.

Winds blow leaves
Skittering across the ground
Making universal sounds.

Rancho Santiago College
Slumbering, waiting.
There seems to be scant fear
Of a war in a far away place.

These children of another war,
Is it so easy to forget?
Like watching leaves
Drop from winter trees,
Then moving on with the eyes
To the young girl by the fountain
With a pensive smile.

In the desert men and women quietly wait.
Is *Crito* right
Again?

THE PRAYER

I pray that as I stand
In this foreign land
I know my enemy
As my brother.

I know that his faith, like mine
Is true to his God,
His family, his home.
That he is there because he too
Trusts in duty.
That someone said,
"Our cause is just."

God I pray
When I aim to kill him
You hold my hand
True, steady.
That my shot is clean,
That he does not suffer needlessly.

We both pray
That in death
Other lives gain meaning.
That this thing we do to each other
Is not in vain,
But seals our bonds as brothers.

29 Jan 91
J

FLAGS

Little flags
Big flags
Waving flags
Somber flags.

Flags folded
Volleys fired
Taps played
Final love.

TWO POEMS

305 Forest Avenue

Through a door
Another land,
The smell of a wild beast,
A camel, Bactrian, I think.
The feel of wool,
Sounds of looms.
Heat, desert, danger.
Take me there
Let me dream freely.

The blues, deep blues
Ancient lapis lazuli, fine filigree silver.
A ring too blue,
Laughing, "Never enough blue."
A nomad's necklace
From the throat, the breast
Of a long ago Queen.

Will its magic bring this wearer,
This God's Handmaiden
Love?

264 Forest Avenue

3" S-3 w/woofer - $499.00
Tiny speakers, beautiful
New Age music, haunting.
While a soundless Proton TV
20", shows the *Wisconsin*
Firing 16" salvos of death.

THE STORM

Queen of Hearts
Warm my wet soul.
I hear the sea
I feel the rain
I see the gulls
Freewheeling, turning
Soaring over waves
Breaking on this shore,
While other waves
Touch other lands
Cleaning, freeing
Making new.
Does this storm
Cleanse the scars
Of a Desert Storm?

27 Feb 91
Camp Pendleton
J

(Untitled)

When you are a professional
It's damn hard
To watch a war
On TV

27 Feb 91
Camp Pendleton
J

(Untitled)

1803 hrs, Pacific Standard Time
This War is over!

Remember the fallen 79.

27 Feb 91
Camp Pendleton
J

THE OTHER WARS

THE TREE

For a year I've gone to the tree.
Fall, leaves red, curling
Different shades of other lives.

As Winter came, colors darken
Falling
Bare limbs, bare soul
Crying, reaching.
Cold sheathing silent pleas.

But in its time,
Within the hardness
Life pulsing, climbing
From roots, to tips of longing arms.
Abundance, leaves greening, growing.

Now, again the red, the staining comes.
Wondering
What is there
When the cycle ends?

(Untitled)

Three steps
   away
A single pool of
   red
How many people
   made that pool?
I see that, but I
   am not a part.
I will care.

Seoul Gardens, Korea
Mar 1984
J

WOMEN WARRIORS

I know that women share the Beast.
That they will fight, kill
Die for a cause.
I have seen them.

They are not always the gentle ones,
The healers.
They too have ferocious fires,
They can lead, are heroes,
Their ways stand proud.
I have seen them.

The Beast that grinds them both
Cares not and
Makes it sadder still.
Wrapping them in bloody blankets,
Families crying out to time,
Praying that it change.
I have seen them.

We are proud of you
Our daughters
Standing with our sons.
Beast, Beast, we love them both.
Always I will see them.

11 November 1991
J

WAR

I survived my war.
My mind scars,
Body scars,
Invisible and life–like maps,
Maps to read if you understand the signs,
The keys.

I survived my war,
With others
Whose memories are today's,
Tomorrow's,
Never History.
Not what you read about.
Not what you think it is.

I survived my war,
I think of those who didn't,
How they died
How I lived.
I smile at memories of you,
I cry at their blank stare.

I survived my war.
It is not hate that binds us,
Each one's time and country asking that they try,
It is the sharing of the fear and love
Strengths we didn't know we had,
You had,
These are the ties.

I survived my war,
I understand and share
Yours.

11 November 1991
J

VANISHING

They fought at places called
Tenaru River, Ledo Road, Buna,
Through hedgerows in France,
On to the Rhine.
In the air, under seas
They killed.
They killed for others imprisoned, dying
At Buchenwald, Baba Yar, Santo Thomas,
On Shanghai streets.
They fought the Savage War
The war for minds, for souls.

Bullets couldn't kill them,
But time is -

(Untitled)

What a beautiful woman
This child of these two races.

Gentle Vietnamese lady
Delicate, moving with grace,
Compassion.
Proud Black man,
Violent, warring past,
Soldier of a Warring presence.

What a beautiful woman
This 20-year-old offspring
Of love?
Of passion?
Wearing her father's skin,
Her mother's eyes.

What a beautiful woman.

LOVE CHILD

She is an enigma.
Her clothes speak of her past,
A warring time and place
She shouldn't know,
But is.

Rising proud above her history
A fierce independence,
Strength from fire,
From passion.
No meekness, no running
Only a gentle assurance.

I am your worst
And will survive.

(Untitled)

Jesus, Helen
It might have been your son.
I remember a quadriplegic,
He stepped on a mine,
The worst kind of death.

But we cheated death
For awhile.
His eyes
I always remember the eyes.
"Why are you doing this to me,
Please, why me?"
We would cut, clean
Start life's blood,
Give breath.
We would say this is good,
This one lived, but I wondered,
Was it honest, was it really good
What we did?
You said "Yes."
Your answer the first I've heard.
An honest mother
A loving mother.
God, I hope it's true.

DACOTAH

Under dark skies,
On rocky fields
We build a future,
A hospital,
A Community of Peace
  and Hope.
A hostile land
  and gentle people.
From a farmer's pasture, now
  a city called Dacotah.
A new road, strength,
  life, sometimes death.

This time we'll do it right.

8 March 89
Honduras
J

STAFF SERGEANT B

He's back in country now.
He really loved it,
The people, the green depths of the jungle.
I think the food had a lot to do with it too.
He was a 91B, a medic.

The other man,
A woodcutter, half Sergeant B's size.
Living up in the mountains
Cutting wood, trying to survive.

They brought him to us
Too late. It had been eight hours,
Another hospital had tried,
We were his last hope. He had bled out.
A cut below the knee, to the bone.
I guess woodcutters do that sometimes.
We tried,
But the doctor said, "Too much time had passed."

I wanted him to go home to his family.
A helicopter would take him,
By ground a day away.
His family would worry.

I watched from a long distance.
Staff Sergeant B
Held him, cleaned his wounds, his body
Washed away the dirt.
It was his son he prepared
Wrapped in our best blankets
To go home.

We carried him out of the hospital
To an ambulance, up to the helipad.
Later that day the Chaplain told me
You shouldn't have let them carry his body out the front door,
"It upset people to see someone dead."
I wanted to hit him.
Twenty years later
They still don't understand.

Staff Sergeant B loves Honduras,
He may never come home.

TO JANE

I knew him,
The soldier on TV,
The face you could never see.

I knew him in Vietnam, Honduras, El Salvador.
He was a boy.
But by War's standards
A seasoned veteran,
A man.

His M−16 or M1A1 or AK−47
Made him the equal
Of men of all sizes,
Of all colors, all faiths, all politics.

Maybe 15,
But probably less.
He'd served two years, they call it drafted,
With two to go.
We called it shanghaied,
And it was for the duration.
Whatever war it was.

His life cruel, mean would be a better word.
His beliefs, his principles, not those of a cause,
But survival, to live, to go home, to go somewhere,
 to something better.

He laughed sometimes, he had friends, maybe a family.
To you he was only a vision on a screen,
A specter.
But I knew him,
Saw those he killed.
Saw him die.
Boys who played in this game, this sport.
Crumpled, missing something, not ever whole again.

You turn off your TV, he ceased to exist.
I knew him.
He's always there.

THE GAME

Soccer players.
Red team
Blue team
Running, smashing, injured
In a game of fun.
Killed in a game of politics.

July 91
ESTADIO DE FUTBOL DE MANAGUA, NICARAGUA
J

DAVID

I drink cerveza
Remembering the private joke,
"Salva Vida" from years ago.
The water would kill me,
Some men would kill me,
History is killing me.

I wonder was it true,
Did he kill those troops,
That Miskito man.
Small price for 16 dead,
A father gone,
Only wanting their land.
A homemade –
What's the word, "grenade"
Yes, that works.

I need shoes
I need food
Take a picture of me,
Send it to my mother.
My real name is David.

David, my son
Are you alive now,
Still running?

I should have helped you more.

July 91
J

MANAGUA HAIKU

This land's steaming rain,
Erases a past's winter Drops.
Dos Killians, please.

                                          Voices right and left,
                                          Summer lights, shimmering heat.
                                          New land confusions.

                    Dark hair, prayer hands,
                    Proud summer smile asking me,
                    "Habla espanol?"

La Casa Fiedler,
Summer resting, years' journeys.
Did you bring me here?

                                          Freedom for your soul,
                                          That's all you want, all you need.
                                          Like you, I cry too.

July 91
J

(Untitled)

One must be careful
How many times
You cross the Jaguar's
Tongue.

July 91
J

PIGS

I am trying.
A song, "I really think we can make it,"
By what's his name.

I want so badly,
But it's hard,
I can't find the answer.

Laughter at the parrots' cage.
Three officious officials impressing a lady
While across the street two pigs rut in the yard.

It is growing dark
For safety's sake
I should move.
But the beer is good
So I stay awhile longer.

July 91
J

THIS WAR

Did this war kill you?
No.
It was the other one,
It just took many years.

July 91
J

AFTER THE WARS

NEAR ONE YEAR

It's storming again.
The clouds are dark,
Rain falls like tears
Down sallow cheeks.

The Gods must be crying,
Saddened that we mortals forget,
Over and over,
And over again.

" THE TRIPLE NICKEL "

Five, Five, Five
It's always there
I see it, know it
Sometimes hear it.

Like the 155's all in a row
Self-Propelled Howitzers
Firing, Firing, Firing
Hitting
               Smashing
                               Concussions
Killing.
Except, they weren't 155's at all.
110's the model box says.
Wrong caliber, wrong name
Wrong memory.

Triple Nickel.
Five, Five, Five Ambulance Company.
A paper tiger, holding names
Not people. No ambulances
No faces. A holding unit
For a Hospital staff.
New Lieutenant,
Learning Honor
Learning Loyalty
Learning Justice.
Proving the First Sergeant lied,
The Commander lied,
Convicting them of some heinous crime,
Some race—related crime.
Where the winner lost,
Where the loser lost,
And the victim sent off
To a place called Vietnam.
Wrong memory.

0558
The mind awakes.
Sweat covered
But not from fear.
Some overactive gland
Fueled by old age causes me to glisten.
Not a war a life ago,
Not memories of valor,
Not faces I can't recall.
Wrong memory.

All these years
Five, Five, Five
A time seen twice a day.
Not luck
But physics.
Not momentous or propitious
But accident
Would dredge up dreams from long ago.
Not accurate,
Distortions through time,
Wrong memory.

0558
1 January 1992
J

"Triple Nickel" MOKI '92

Biography:

Photo by Carrie A. Piela

John Harrell graduated with a BA Degree in Philosophy from San Jose State College. Upon graduation, he began his military career by enlisting in the Hawaiian National Guard. In 1967, he accepted a direct commission as a Medical Service Corps Officer and completed over twenty years active Army service. His assignments included tours of duty in Okinawa, Vietnam (AMERICAL Division 1969-70), Colorado, Texas, Massachusetts, Oklahoma and California. He also completed temporary assignments in Germany, and Central and South America.

Upon his retirement in 1989, he began studying and writing poetry seriously. His poetry has been published in national and college anthologies, *The Journal of the Gulf War*, *The Orange County Register* and the *Los Angeles Times*. For him, poetry is a way to paint life's pictures. The words and sounds are the colors and images.

Philip L. "Moki" Martin started painting in 1987 after a bicycle accident cut short a 23-year career as a Naval SEAL Officer. Moki spent two and a half years in Vietnam and travelled extensively in the conduct of naval special warfare. He graduated from art school at San Diego State with a BA degree in Applied Arts and Science. Moki has won art awards locally and nationally, including several first place awards in the National Veterans' Art Exhibitions. Presently, he is preparing a Masters of Fine Art portfolio to be submitted to a southern California university. For Janet Cooling, artist and professor, San Diego State University, "Moki has already lead a remarkable life with plenty of material to fuel his creativity...He has always touched me with his honesty, continuing openness to life and art, and an eagerness to grapple with ideas...Moki is a profound artist."

Photo by Joel B. Martin

First printed in an edition for the trade and in a limited hardbound edition of 274 copies, numbered and signed by the poet and the artist. Copies in an additional collectors' run are lettered A through Z and are signed by the author, artist, and editor. These lettered copies include two additional poems and one additional art work in color.
Printed in 11 point Helvetica, on 65–pound Cougar Cover, Vellum Finish.

2/274